T0266699

SPOTLIGHT ON NATURE
ALLIGATOR

MELISSA GISH

CREATIVE EDUCATION · CREATIVE PAPERBACKS

Published by Creative Education and Creative Paperbacks
P.O. Box 227, Mankato, Minnesota 56002
Creative Education and Creative Paperbacks are imprints
of The Creative Company
www.thecreativecompany.us

Design and production
by Chelsey Luther
Art direction by Rita Marshall
Printed in the United States of America

Photographs by Alamy (All Canada Photos, Joe Blossom, Iakov Filimonov,
jb886, Papilio, RooM the Agency, Tetra Images), Dreamstime (Christopher
Elwell, Isselee), Getty Images (Christophe Lehenaff/Photononstop, jared
lloyd/Moment), iStockphoto (aoldman, Canon_Bob, KenCanning, stock-
tributor, zhnger), Shutterstock (Africa Studio, Eric Gevaert, Vladislav T.
Jirousek, Mammut Vision, Marc Pletcher, Jeroen Visser)

Library of Congress Cataloging-in-Publication Data
Names: Gish, Melissa, author.
Title: Alligator / Melissa Gish.
Series: Spotlight on nature.
Includes index.
Summary: A detailed chronology of developmental milestones drives this life
study of alligators, including their habitats, physical features, and conserva-
tion measures taken to protect these semiaquatic reptiles.
Identifiers: LCCN 2019060158 / ISBN 978-1-64026-336-9 (hardcover) /
ISBN 978-1-62832-868-4 (pbk) / ISBN 978-1-64000-478-8 (eBook)
Subjects: LCSH: Alligators—Juvenile literature.
Classification: LCC QL666.C925 G554 2021 / DDC 597.98/4—dc23

First Edition HC 9 8 7 6 5 4 3 2 1
First Edition PBK 9 8 7 6 5 4 3 2 1

CONTENTS

MEET THE FAMILY

American Alligators of
Big Cypress Swamp   4

LIFE BEGINS   7

Featured Family
Welcome to the World   8
First Meal   10

**EARLY
ADVENTURES**   13

Featured Family
Look Who's Diving   14
Give It a Try   16

LIFE LESSONS   19

Featured Family
This Is How It's Done   20
Practice Makes Perfect   22

**ALLIGATOR
SPOTTING**   25

Family Album Snapshots   **28**
Words to Know   **30**
Learn More   **31**
Index   **32**

AMERICAN ALLIGATORS
of Big Cypress Swamp

Near Florida's southwestern coast lies a sprawling wetland about the size of Rhode Island. In Big Cypress National Preserve, bald cypress trees tower more than 100 feet (30.5 m) tall. In their dappled shade, orchids and **epiphytes** grow. Ferns blanket the ground. Alligators, water snakes, and river otters share the early September floodwater. Long-legged herons wade, watching for fish. The coming dry season will invite panthers, bobcats, and black bears deeper into the swamp.

On a bank, safely above the waterline, sits a mound of soil, leaves, and sticks. It is about five feet (1.5 m) in diameter and three feet (0.9 m) high. A female American alligator has been guarding the mound—and the 37 eggs buried beneath. For the past 65 days, the rotting vegetation has created heat to **incubate** the eggs. Now a low chirp emanates from the mound. Then another. The eggs are hatching.

Egg tooth

Inside their eggs, baby alligators develop a
thorny projection on the tip of their snout. This
tooth is used to rip through the tough eggshell.
Within a week of hatching, the tooth is resorbed.

CHAPTER ONE
LIFE BEGINS

Alligators are semiaquatic reptiles. They breathe air and live on land but spend much of their time in the water. Like all reptiles, alligators cannot generate their own body heat. To warm up, they lie in the sun to absorb heat. When they need to cool off, they lie in the shade or submerge themselves in water. By adjusting the amount of air in their lungs, alligators can float or sink at will. When an alligator goes underwater, its body seals up tight like a submarine. Folds of skin close over its ears. Muscles squeeze its nostrils shut. Its tongue, which is attached to the bottom of its mouth, works like a plug to block its throat.

BIG CYPRESS SWAMP ALLIGATOR MILESTONES

DAY ①

- Hatch from eggs
- Black skin marked with yellow bands
- Weight: 2.4 ounces (68 g)
- Length: 8 inches (20.3 cm)

 FEATURED FAMILY

Welcome to the World

In Big Cypress Swamp, the baby alligators call out with croaks and grunts. Their mother gently claws at the nest to uncover her offspring. The babies, called hatchlings, scurry toward the water. About a third of the eggs has not hatched. With great care, the mother alligator uses her teeth to break the leathery shell of each unhatched egg. Babies emerge from some of them. Soon, 27 hatchlings are gathered around their mother in the water. Some ride on her head. She will do her best to keep them safe in the coming months.

Chinese alligator
5 feet (1.5 m)

American alligator
13 feet (4 m)

There are two alligator species. The American alligator inhabits wetlands and swamps of the southern United States, from Texas to North Carolina. The Chinese alligator is found only in parts of the Yangtze River basin in eastern China. Male American alligators average about 13 feet (4 m) in length and may weigh more than 800 pounds (363 kg). Females rarely grow more than 10 feet (3 m) long. The smaller Chinese alligator measures less than 5 feet (1.5 m) in length and weighs no more than 90 pounds (40.8 kg).

CLOSE-UP
Alligator toes

Alligators have five toes on each front foot. Three of the toes have sharp claws for digging burrows and nests. Each back foot has four toes connected with fleshy skin. Three of these toes also have claws.

 MONTHS

▸ Hunting by mother's side
▸ Weight: 7.5 pounds (3.4 kg)
▸ Length: 12 inches (30.5 cm)

Alligators live alone. They avoid each other, except during courtship and mating season, from April to June. Like most reptiles, alligators reproduce by laying eggs. A female uses her snout and claws to rake up a mounded nest on high ground. She lays up to 70 eggs, each a little more than 3 inches (7.6 cm) long. Then she buries the eggs. About three weeks later, the amount of heat within the nest determines the gender of the babies. At temperatures above 91 °F (32.8 °C), embryos develop into males. Those that incubate below 87 °F (30.6 °C) develop as females. Temperatures in between produce some of each. Curled up inside their eggs, the babies will grow to be six to eight inches (15.2–20.3 cm) long. Their mother will protect the nest from snakes, raccoons, and other predators.

FEATURED FAMILY

First Meal

With their mother keeping close watch, the Big Cypress hatchlings swim among slender blades of knotted spikerush. They hatched with a mouthful of needle-like teeth and instinctively snap at anything that moves. Swarms of mayflies skim and bounce over the water's surface, attracting hungry golden topminnows. Sensing this movement, the hatchlings dive toward the small fish. Most are successful in their hunt and swallow the topminnows whole. As the fish flee, the other hatchlings must settle for plucking snails off the spikerush stems.

(1) YEAR

- Capturing prey up to 3 pounds (1.4 kg)
- Weight: 30 pounds (13.6 kg)
- Length: 24 inches (61 cm)

Replaceable teeth

Adult alligators have 74 to 80 teeth suited to gripping prey. As teeth wear down, new ones emerge to replace them. An alligator may go through 2,000 to 3,000 teeth in its lifetime.

CHAPTER TWO
EARLY ADVENTURES

An adult alligator's skin is mostly bite-proof. Its body is covered by thick, scaly skin. Bony ridges under the skin of the back and tail are called scutes. Young alligators do not have scutes. Yellow bands on their dark skin provide camouflage from predators. When hatchlings sense danger, they croak and grunt. Their mother protects them as well as she can, but hatchlings face many threats. Herons may pluck them from above, while largemouth bass may gulp them from underwater. Snapping turtles, otters, bobcats, and even large snakes hunt young alligators. A mother alligator keeps her offspring close for the first five months of their lives. As they grow, the group, called a pod, becomes more adventurous, though they continue to remain near their mother for up to two years.

2 YEARS	3 YEARS
▸ Begin swimming farther away ▸ Return to mother at night	▸ Pod disbands ▸ Juveniles leave mother's territory ▸ Able to crush large turtles and catch small deer

Within their first year, hatchlings may grow to 24 inches (61 cm) in length. Over the next three years, juveniles may grow another 12 inches (30.5 cm) per year. By the age of four, their yellow bands have faded, and scutes have developed. Now their only remaining predators are larger alligators and, in the U.S., American crocodiles. Alligators can swim fast—up to 20 miles (32.2 km) per hour. To swim, they tuck their feet against their body and swish their tail back and forth. Young alligators cannot outswim larger alligators, so their only defense is to avoid being seen by patrolling adults.

CLOSE-UP
Vision

Alligators have good vision. They can see in all directions except right behind them. A nictitating (*NIK-tih-tayt-ing*) membrane closes over each eye. This inner eyelid allows the alligator to see while underwater.

—————————— FEATURED FAMILY ——————————

Look Who's Diving

In Big Cypress, two of the young alligators ventured too far from their mother and were eaten by a snapping turtle. Several others will be lost later this year. The remaining juveniles are now six months old. Floating in the water, they can sense the movement of crayfish in the mud below them. The juveniles use their webbed hind feet and tails to swim downward, but they do not yet weigh enough to submerge for long without great effort. They swim to the shore, where they swallow mouthfuls of pebbles. The extra weight is just enough to help the young alligators sink. On the muddy bottom of the swamp, they snatch the fat crayfish.

4 YEARS	6 YEARS
▸ Skin dark green, yellow bands gone	▸ Establish permanent territories
▸ Weight: 70 pounds (31.8 kg)	▸ Able to fight or escape larger alligators
▸ Length: 4.5 feet (1.4 m) long	

— FEATURED FAMILY —

Give It a Try

At almost 2 years old, the 13 surviving Big Cypress alligators are now big enough to capture small prey on land. Just after sunset, one alligator floats among beakrush, its face mere inches from shore. An immature muskrat ventures along the muddy bank, hungry for the plants. The muskrat does not see the dangerous predator lurking nearby. In an instant, the young alligator thrusts forward, grabbing for the muskrat's small head. But its aim is off, and the muskrat leaps away. This alligator needs more practice.

Adult alligators can LEAP STRAIGHT UP as high as their BODY LENGTH.

8 YEARS

- Males are mature
- Male weight: 170 pounds (77.1 kg)
- Male length: 6.5 feet (2 m) long

10 YEARS

- Females are mature
- Female weight: 150 pounds (68 kg)
- Female length: 6.5 feet (2 m) long

CLOSE-UP
Death roll

Alligators cannot chew, but some prey is too big to swallow whole. With prey trapped in its jaws, an alligator will spin over and over underwater. Called a "death roll," this motion can break off smaller pieces to eat.

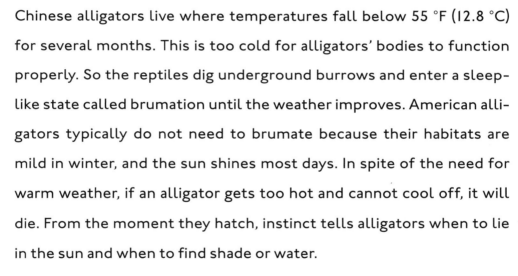

CHAPTER THREE

LIFE LESSONS

Chinese alligators live where temperatures fall below 55 °F (12.8 °C) for several months. This is too cold for alligators' bodies to function properly. So the reptiles dig underground burrows and enter a sleep-like state called brumation until the weather improves. American alligators typically do not need to brumate because their habitats are mild in winter, and the sun shines most days. In spite of the need for warm weather, if an alligator gets too hot and cannot cool off, it will die. From the moment they hatch, instinct tells alligators when to lie in the sun and when to find shade or water.

Most adult alligators live alone in an established territory. An alligator does not share this area with other alligators. Unless its territory is destroyed or a stronger alligator kicks it out, the alligator will stay at this home base its entire life. When a young alligator leaves its

 YEARS

  ▸ Males find their first mates
  ▸ Weight: 250 pounds (113 kg)
  ▸ Length: 8 feet (2.4 m) long

 YEARS

  ▸ Females mate for the first time
  ▸ Build first nests and lay eggs

This Is How It's Done

The Big Cypress alligators have been sunning themselves on the bank. Feeling warm, some move off to the shade, while two of the young alligators slip into the water. They sense vibrations and dip below the surface. A school of bluegills is heading toward them. The alligators are now patient hunters. Instead of charging forward, they float, perfectly still, and wait. Unaware, the fish swim straight to the alligators. With a swift jerk of the head and snap of the jaws, each alligator captures a fish.

Gator holes

As dry season approaches, alligators clear vegetation from rocky depressions. When wetlands dry up, these "gator holes" remain filled with water. They provide relief to many animals that sneak in for a drink.

pod, it must find a place to establish a territory. Sometimes juveniles travel far from where they hatched. Females usually prefer marshy areas that provide nesting material and protection for offspring. Males often choose areas with access to open water. During the spring mating season, males visit females' territories.

Communication is essential to alligator survival. As youngsters, alligators vocalize to their mother. To attract mates and deter rivals, adult alligators forcefully exhale from the nostrils to make a deep huffing noise called a bellow. During several days of mating, a pair of alligators will perform an activity called head slapping. Each partner rests its lower jaw on the surface of the water and then slaps down its upper jaw, causing a loud pop as the jaws meet and hit the water. Like all reptiles, alligators develop more quickly in heat than in cold. American alligators are fully mature when they reach about six feet (1.8 m) in length. This could be anytime from ages 7 to 12. Since reptiles do not grow during brumation, Chinese alligators may not mature for up to nine years.

(30) YEARS

- ▸ Growth ceases
- ▸ Weight: 700 pounds (318 kg)
- ▸ Length: 11 feet (3.4 m) long

Growth rate

Alligators grow fastest when temperatures are between 85 and 91 °F (29.4 to 32.8 °C). When the temperature drops below 70 °F (21.1 °C), alligators stop eating—and stop growing.

FEATURED FAMILY

Practice Makes Perfect

It is time for the remaining Big Cypress alligators to leave the safety of the pod and venture off alone. The 12 subadults will move slowly and try to avoid the territories of larger alligators. At night, they will float with only their eyes and nostrils above the water's surface, prepared to ambush unwary prey. The young alligators may eat a quarter of their body weight in one meal, growing a little stronger and larger every day. Some will not reach maturity, but some will live to be 40, 50, and even 70 years old.

Some alligators live to be SEVENTY years old.

(50) **YEARS**

▸ End of lives

CHAPTER FOUR
ALLIGATOR SPOTTING

Of the two alligator species, the Chinese alligator is more threatened. Earth's last remaining wild Chinese alligators exist only in a handful of ponds, streams, and wetlands along the lower Yangtze River in the Anhui Province of China. With fewer than 120 left in the wild, this alligator is one of the most endangered reptiles on the planet. As farms and cities expand, the alligator's habitat continues to shrink.

Two breeding centers in China are responsible for keeping Chinese alligators alive—at least in captivity. The Anhui Research Center for Chinese Alligator Reproduction (ARCCAR) was founded in 1979. Shortly thereafter, it established a large reserve. Starting with 212 alligators captured in the wild, the center is now home to more than 15,000 Chinese alligators. In Zhejiang Province, about 82 acres (33.2 ha) of wetland has been set aside as an alligator reserve. The reserve, which had just 118 alligators in 1998, now holds about 5,500 Chinese alligators. Scientists predict that the wild Chinese alligator population will be wiped out by 2025, but researchers are determined to keep this species safe. They hope to one day repopulate wild places with Chinese alligators.

The American alligator nearly suffered the same fate as its Chinese cousin. In addition to destroying alligator habitat, people hunted alligators for their skin and meat. By the 1960s, the American alligator population had dropped from 7 million to about 700,000. This concerned wildlife experts, and in 1962, the federal government banned the hunting of alligators. Over the next 20 years, the alligator population more than doubled. Today, alligators are hunted as game animals, but licenses are limited annually.

Roughly 2 million people visit the Florida Everglades and Big Cypress National Preserve each year. Many specifically head into the swamp to see wild alligators. Piloting airboats, expert guides take passengers deep into alligator territory. In brackish coastal waters, tourists might be lucky enough to also catch a glimpse of the American crocodile. These alligator relatives live mostly in Mexico and Central and South America, but scientists believe there could be up to 1,200 American crocodiles living in Florida. They get along just fine with their alligator cousins and sometimes even share territory. Continued study of alligators and their needs is important to protecting and preserving these amazing animals for the future.

SNAPSHOTS

As of 2020, the largest **American alligator** on record was caught in Alabama in 2014. It measured 15.75 feet (4.8 m) long and weighed 1,011.5 pounds (459 kg).

In its native land, the **Chinese alligator** is called *tu long*, which means "muddy dragon." It likely inspired the first tales of Chinese dragons more than 7,000 years ago.

American crocodiles are typically longer and heavier than **American alligators**, but they have a narrower snout and fewer teeth.

Chubbs, an **American alligator**, frequents the Buffalo Creek Golf Course in Palmetto, Florida. Because he ignores golfers, no one has asked that he be relocated.

The **Indian gharial**, an alligator cousin, lives in India and Nepal. Its slender jaws and interlocking teeth are specialized for catching fish.

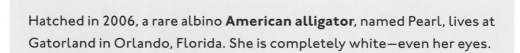

Hatched in 2006, a rare albino **American alligator**, named Pearl, lives at Gatorland in Orlando, Florida. She is completely white—even her eyes.

The critically endangered **Siamese crocodile** was the inspiration for the Malaysian folk tale about Sang Buaya, a crocodile who gets tricked by a mouse deer.

European tales of fire-breathing dragons can be traced back to **Chinese alligators**, which were described by the Italian explorer Marco Polo in the 13th century.

An alligator relative, the **Cuban crocodile**, has pebbly black, yellow, and cream-colored skin. This has led to the nickname "pearly crocodile."

Bouya Blan, whose name means "white fog," is a rare leucistic **American alligator**. He is housed at Gator Spot in Orlando, Florida.

The alligator's smallest relative is the **Cuvier's dwarf caiman**. It lives in rivers and lakes in the Amazon basin and grows to about 15 pounds (6.8 kg).

The largest alligator cousin on record is a 20.25-foot-long (6.2 m) **saltwater crocodile**. Captured in the Philippines in 2011, he was suspected of eating humans.

American alligators at North Carolina's Shallotte River Swamp Park endure cold winters by brumating underwater with only their snouts protruding from the ice.

WORDS to Know

airboats — boats powered by airplane propellers and used to travel through shallow water

brackish — containing a mixture of salt and fresh water

camouflage — the ability to hide by blending in with a given environment

captivity — living in a place from which escape is not possible

endangered — at risk of dying out completely

epiphytes — plants that grow on other plants without taking nutrients from them

incubate — to keep eggs warm and protected until it is time for them to hatch

leucistic — describing an animal with blue eyes and pale or white skin because of a lack of pigment

nictitating membrane — clear tissue that sweeps across the eye from side to side to clean and protect the eye

species — a group of living beings with shared characteristics and the ability to reproduce with one another

LEARN MORE

Books

Hirsch, Rebecca H. *American Alligators: Armored Roaring Reptiles*.
Minneapolis: Lerner, 2016.

Marsh, Laura. *Alligators and Crocodiles*. Washington, D.C.: National
Geographic Society, 2015.

Ouchley, Kelby. *American Alligator: Ancient Predator in the Modern World*.
Gainesville, Fla.: University Press of Florida, 2013.

Websites

"American Alligator." Smithsonian's National Zoo & Conservation Biology
Institute. https://nationalzoo.si.edu/animals/american-alligator.

"American Crocodile and Alligator." Defenders of Wildlife. https://defenders
.org/wildlife/american-crocodile-and-alligator.

Brain, Marshall. "How Alligators Work." How Stuff Works. https://animals
.howstuffworks.com/reptiles/alligator.htm.

Documentaries

Mesker, Ben. "Wild Florida." *How to Do Florida*, season 8, episode 4. Crawford
Entertainment, 2017.

Neal, Cynthia. *Alligators: More Than Meets the Eye*. Kiawah Conservancy, 2016.

Stoltzfus, Elam. *Big Cypress Swamp: The Western Everglades*. Live Oak Production Group, 2009.

Visit

EVERGLADES NATIONAL PARK

On tours led by park rangers, visitors can see alligators in the wild year round.

40001 State Road 9336
Homestead, FL 33034

GATORLAND

Get up-close to American alligators at this 110-acre (44.5 ha) preserve.

14501 S. Orange Blossom Trail
Orlando, FL 32837

JEAN LAFITTE SWAMP AND AIRBOAT TOURS

Guided airboat rides take visitors into swamps teeming with wildlife.

6601 Leo Kerner Lafitte Parkway
Marrero, LA 70072

SMITHSONIAN'S NATIONAL ZOO & CONSERVATION BIOLOGY INSTITUTE

See Chinese and American alligators in the Reptile Discovery Center.

3001 Connecticut Avenue NW
Washington, D.C. 20008

INDEX

burrows 9, 19

China 9, 25

conservation measures 4, 25–26, 28, 29
   protected areas 4, 25, 26, 28, 29
   research centers 25

eggs 4, 6, 8, 10

eyes 14, 22, 28

feet 8, 9, 10, 14

food 10, 12, 14, 16, 18, 20, 22

jaws 10, 18, 20, 21

life spans 22

mating 10, 21

movement 7, 8, 10, 14, 16, 18, 20, 22

nests 4, 8, 9, 10, 21

offspring 4, 6, 8, 10, 13, 14, 16, 20, 21, 22

pods 13, 21, 22

populations 25, 26

skin 13, 14, 26

snouts 6, 10, 28, 29

species 4, 9, 19, 21, 25, 26, 28, 29

tails 13, 14, 16

teeth 8, 10, 12, 28

territories 19, 21, 22

threats 10, 13, 14, 25, 26

United States 4, 9, 14, 26, 28, 29

vocalizations 4, 8, 13, 21